COFFEE BREAK CREATIVITY grande!

101 WAYS TO SPARK YOUR CREATIVITY

Maria Gatling

Slow Burn Books

A special thank you to my friend
and publisher, Linda Battson.
Her expertise and guidance has taken me
to another level of achievement.
Her many talents and ability to visualize
my projects give me hope and inspiration
to continue my work.

Coffee Break Creativity - Grande!
© Copyright 2018 by Maria Gatling. All rights
reserved. Printed in the United States of America.
No part of this book may be used or reproduced in
any manner whatsoever without written permission.

ISBN 978-0-9893794-6-5

Cover design and consulting: Nicole Nixon Design.
Editing consulting and publishing: Linda Battson Art
and Slow Burn Books.

to you who are reading this...

you can do this.

Somewhere along the road from childhood to adulthood, we tend to lose our creative spark.

Ultimately though, most of us seek fulfillment and joy, but mindless meetings and hectic schedules can damper our creative flame.

This notebook was made to help you cultivate your own spark and remind you of your creative awesomeness.

Maria

How to use this notebook

With each entry, take the time to jot down some ideas, notes, and sketches. Don't forget to use color! Simply let your mind release all that comes from the prompts on these pages.

If the prompt suggests that you watch a TED talk, take a few minutes to do a search and write down some titles or topics to view later.

If the prompt suggests you put together a simple presentation, take a few minutes to write down some possible topics including the how and when.

Use the blank pages to write, sketch, draw, and expand on any ideas you have from these prompts.

Write *big*, be **bold**, and please have *fun*.

1 list 3 good things
that happened to you recently.

2 make a list of
your favorite...

3 Look up the *lyrics* to one of
your favorite songs and write
your favorite verse here.

"

4 Turn these **3 *circles*** into recognizable objects.

○ ○ ○

5 Get **3 *paint chips*** from the hardware store that you think go well together. Cut ***shapes*** to your liking and use those paint chips to create a card or quick piece of *art*.

6 Put together a ***simple presentation*** for a team meeting presenting on a subject you love...film, art, technology, food, sports, etc. Encourage other team members to participate. What subject would you choose?

7 what if...

8 create a coloring book

Gather pattern ideas from a piece of clothing you own, an image out of a magazine, or other sources of inspiration. Expand on those by drawing them in a notebook. Continue to fill your notebook with other sources of inspiration. Grab your favorite colors and get going.

9 my favorite color is:

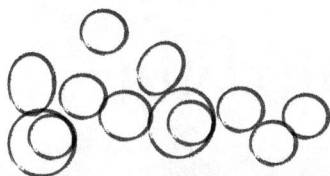

10 travel tip

light up your night

and

Don't forget to

boogie.

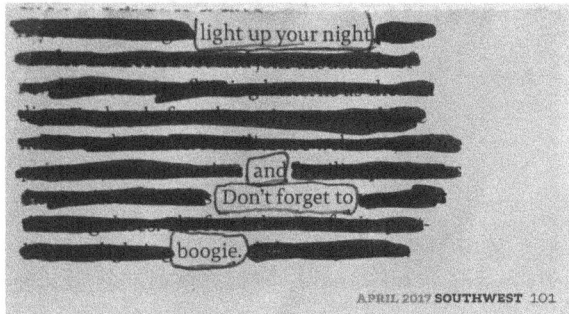

Use the airline magazine to create *black out poems* on your flight. Share on social media and tag the airline.

11 volunteer at your favorite charity

12

Take your meeting out of the office. Enjoy a walk around the grounds or find an interesting place nearby to gather with other employees.

"

13 People ask "Where do you see yourself in 5 years?" How about, "Where do you see yourself at the end of today?" Write that down. What will you accomplish, big or small, for work or pleasure?

14 write a love note

15 one thing I want to accomplish in the next month:

16 create something and sell it

A photograph, a hand sewn item, a drawing—post it for sale on social media. Talk to your local coffee shop and get the word out.

17 create a piece of original art

and hang it in your home or give it as a gift to someone you care about.

18 buy a piece of original art

and hang it in your home. Get to know the artist and the story behind the art.

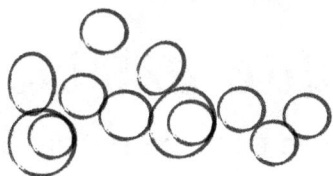

19 write a mini-saga

Write approximately 50 words about yourself and share it with co-workers and friends. Include a sketch or photo.

20 watch a documentary

about a famous artist.

21 travel tip

Take a "staycation" in your own city. Book the hotel and make reservations for dining at a restaurant you've always wanted to try. Attend a concert. Use a ride service instead of driving.

"

22 unplug for a day
No social media, no texting, no internet.

23 schedule family time
Organize a family gathering. Invite them over for a potluck dinner or make reservations for everyone at your favorite restaurant.

24 plant something you can eat

25 count your blessings

List some of those here.

26 read a classic novel with a friend

What classic novel would you read and which friend would you read it with?

27 do absolutely nothing for a day

except for maybe reading that classic novel you're supposed to be reading with a friend.

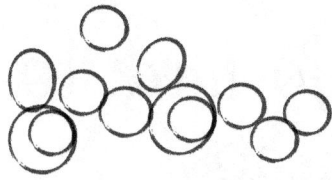

28 go back to school

Find a class on something you've never tried before. Dance, yoga, musical instrument, etc. What class would you like to take?

29 go to the park and swing

30 exercise daily

If you do exercise daily, what is your routine?

“

31 discover your purpose

Finish this sentence:
I want to be…

32 go to bed earlier

Sleep more.

33 travel tip

Explore new places and areas by foot. Walk where the locals do and photograph a theme unique to that city—fashion, architecture, food, etc.

34 be kind and generous

35 create a "city book"

Photograph your favorite places in your city. Use an online service like Chatbooks or Shutterfly to create your own coffee table photo book. List a few places to photograph:

36 declutter your home

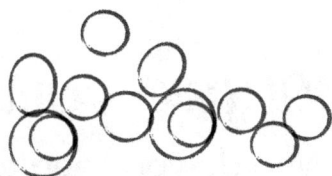

37 forgive someone
Who do you need to forgive?

38 play catch with a child
Do you have children, grandchildren, nieces or nephews? Put it on your schedule to make sure a play date happens.

39 sing!
Sing out loud in the car, in the shower, or anywhere. Do you have a favorite song you like to sing?

40 buy a card
and alter the image by
drawing or gluing
something funny on it.
Send it to a friend.

41 give away
something
valuable
you own

42 spend 5 minutes
every night
stretching

43 spend time outdoors daily

44 attend art events
Go to a museum, art gallery, concert, and a play. List a few.

45 watch a TED talk
Make a list of a few to watch soon.

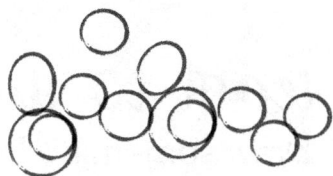

46 learn to draw

Draw something here.

47 learn a new language

Speak a little every day.

48 learn to play a musical instrument

"

49 *carry a notebook* with you at all times. Inspiration is everywhere!

50 Create the kind of day you want. *Wake up*, stretch and write down what you want out of your day. Don't check email or do anything that adds stress first thing in the morning. What would your perfect day look like?

51 *Write* someone a *sweet, random note*. Put it in their car, lunch box, or backpack. What would you write?

52 give a talk

Prepare a talk about your work expertise for a group of students at a local school.

53 read fiction novels

What's on your list?

54 write a short poem

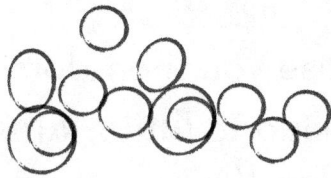

55 Use your non-dominant hand to *write, draw,* or *doodle* a message to a friend or co-worker. Practice here.

56 *Create* a *vision board* for your team and hang it in a common area. Once a week, have everyone *contribute* an *image* to the board and have discussions about the *images*.

57 *Play word games that challenge you*

"

58 Define who you are or what you do in *7 words*.

59 meeting notes
Draw and *doodle* as part of your meeting notes.

60 learn Tai Chi
Practice it.

61 create space

Designate a space in your home that you can call your own. Use it to write, draw, and create art.

62 start an art group

Create art, collaborate, exhibit, and learn from each other. Who would you invite?

63 be excited!

Have something to wake up for and be excited about. What is it that excites you?

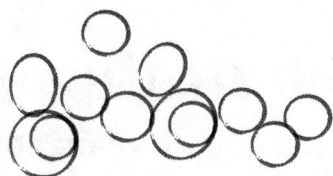

64 set creative goals

List a couple of creative projects that you want to begin and put a completion date on them.

65 plan a costume party at your home

66

Design a business card for yourself based on a business you think would be fun. This can be total fantasy. Begin with a quick sketch right here.

"

67 breathe deeply

Close your eyes and take 5 deep breaths.

68 go to a farmers' market

Take photos, buy fresh produce and talk to the farmers about their foods.

69

Go to the mall and try on clothes you would not typically wear.

70 say thank you

Make your own thank you card for a friend, client or co-worker. Who would you send it to?

71 sketch one small thing every day

Start here.

72 take a walk

without your phone.

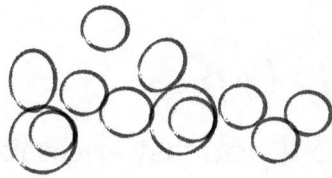

73 listen
to a podcast and take notes. Share with a friend.

74 be well
Be proactive about your health and well-being.

75 show your work
Exhibit, present, or simply share on social media.

"

76 *Put your headphones on*
and play your favorite songs.

77 *dance!*
Dance alone, with your
family, friends, or anyone
you love.

78 Keep a notepad close by
when *watching* television
so you can write down any
ideas you get.

79 Go on a *photo walk-about* in your office building or neighborhood.

80 *write at least one sentence in a notebook every day*
Start here.

81 Keep up with technology as much as possible. Learn to use apps that reinforce *creativity*.

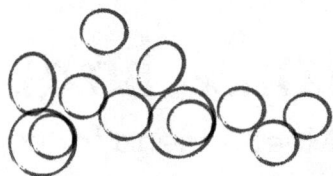

82 coffee break art

Meet a friend for coffee and bring a pencil and notebook. Take 15 minutes to sketch your surroundings and share your art with each other.

83 Draw a picture of someone...with your eyes closed.

84 travel

Plan a trip and put images on your dream board. Continue to add details as the trip evolves.

"

85 play dress up

Go into your own closet —
mix and match items you
haven't worn in awhile.

86 create a collage using old magazines

87 old-style inspiration

Go to the bookstore and look
through magazines you've
never heard of. Write down
and sketch any ideas that
come to you.

La 2 20   N. 2

maria

88 create a fun and playful self-portrait

89 index card walk

Grab a pencil and index card. Go on a short walk and use the index card to write down any ideas and thoughts you have while you are on a walk. Tape it down in this notebook after your walk.

90

Don't over-plan creative projects. Leave room for *amazing*.

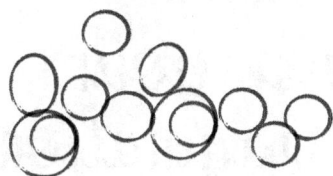

91 use your imagination

Re-create someone else's art. Experiment with art supplies you have and allow your own style to come through. Your "mistakes" will lead to your own personal style.

92 rearrange everything on your bookshelves

93

Enjoy the *creative process* and try not to focus on the end result.

"

94 create a photo book recapping your year

95 Pick a *friend* and tell them 3 things you really **love** about them. Write it out here.

96 Make up your own "mafia" name and write it here. Mine is *"Cupcake."*

No. 2

maria

97 list some of your skills

98

Take 5 minutes to do a photo shoot of something in your daily routine, such as your morning coffee, kids getting ready for school, preparing dinner, checking the mail.

99 fall in love

with your boyfriend, girlfriend, husband, wife, friends, babies. Fall in love with your life, your method, your journey.

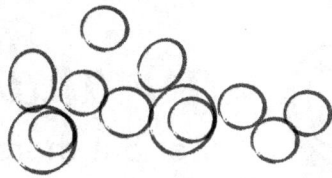

100 go and do!

Get out there and try some of these tips. You can't mess up.

101 Color

all 101 numbers in this book.

Share pictures of your creativity

Tag **@mariagatling**
@beinspiredtocreate
#coffeebreakcreativity

About the Writer

Maria Gatling is a visual artist whose drive is to spread the love of creativity.

As a "Creativity Facilitator," she helps others embrace creativity in everyday life. Maria's books and workshops encourage people to use simple actions to tap into their creative side.

Maria lives in the Austin, TX area with her husband, children, and grandkids.

My favorite coffee is a smooth cappuccino or a double shot latte.

Maria would love to hear how this book has helped to build more enjoyment in your days:

marygatling@mac.com. / mariagatling.com

www.ingramcontent.com/pod-product-compliance
Lightning Source LLC
LaVergne TN
LVHW091207080426
835509LV00006B/883